HOW TO CARE FOR A LEATHERBACK TURTLE

THE ULTIMATE GUIDE TO KEEPING THEM AS PETS

DR MORRIS HART

Table of Contents

Introduction

Although owning a leatherback turtle as a pet has its advantages, there are also big obligations involved. We'll cover all you need to know about keeping these intriguing animals as pets in this extensive guide.

1. Comprehending Leatherback Turtles

The largest sea turtles, known as Leatherbacks (Dermochelys coriacea), are distinguished by having leathery shells rather than hard, bony plates. These magnificent reptiles are a sight to behold, reaching lengths of up to 7 feet and weights exceeding 2,000 pounds.

2. Legal Aspects to Take into Account

It's important to become aware of the laws governing the ownership of leatherback turtles before you take on the adventure of being their owner. Because of their endangered status, these turtles are legally protected in many areas. Make sure you acquire any licenses or permits needed in order to keep them as pets.

3. Moral Aspects to Take into Account

Even though it could be permissible in some places to keep leatherback turtles as pets, it's important to think about the moral ramifications of doing so. As highly specialized marine animals, leatherback turtles have intricate needs that might be difficult to satisfy in captivity. Consider carefully whether you can provide the right atmosphere and care to ensure its wellbeing before getting one as a pet.

4. Particular Requirements of Leatherback Turtles

For leatherback turtles to flourish in captivity, certain conditions must be satisfied. Since they are cold-blooded reptiles, their body temperature is controlled by outside heat sources. They also need access to both land and water since they come ashore to nest and spend the majority of their life in the ocean.

5. Creating the Ideal Environment

It is essential to your leatherback turtle's health and welfare to provide an appropriate habitat for it. It's crucial to have a roomy tank or cage that allows you to swim and sunbathe. A basking area with a heat lamp to simulate the natural sunshine they would receive in the wild should be provided, and the water temperature should be kept within the ideal range.

6. How to Feed a Leatherback Turtle

For your leatherback turtle to stay healthy, it must eat a balanced diet. While they mostly eat jellyfish in the nature, several diets can be provided in captivity, such as fish, squid, shrimp, and commercially made turtle pellets. To guarantee they get all the nutrients they require, it's critical to offer a diversified diet.

7. Keeping Your Health at Its Best

Your leatherback turtle's health must be regularly monitored via veterinarian visits. Nutritional deficits, respiratory infections, and shell infections are common health problems in captive turtles. A healthy diet, adequate care, and a clean environment can all aid in preventing the development of numerous health issues.

8. Managing and Getting Along Safely

Even though it could be tempting to handle your leatherback turtle, you must use caution and regard for its welfare when doing so. Given their strong swimming ability, these turtles should only be handled carefully to prevent stress or harm. Handle them only as much as is required, such as when cleaning their cage or bringing them to the vet.

9. Breeding-Related Issues

The process of breeding leatherback turtles in captivity is difficult and complicated, requiring considerable preparation and forethought. Be sure you have the knowledge, tools, and licenses needed to responsibly breed these turtles before attempting to do so. Consulting with seasoned breeders or conservation groups can yield invaluable advice and assistance.

10. In summary

For committed and informed reptile enthusiasts, keeping a leatherback turtle as a pet can be a rewarding experience. You can make sure that your leatherback turtle thrives in captivity by being aware of their particular needs, giving them the right care and enrichment, and honoring their natural habits. Pet ownership must, however, be approached thoughtfully and with a dedication to the welfare of these amazing animals.

Chapter 1

Recognizing the Particular Requirements of Leatherback Turtles

Amazing animals, leatherback turtles have unique needs that distinguish them from other reptiles. The largest of all sea turtles, they have developed particular adaptations to help them survive in the open ocean, where they encounter several obstacles. The special requirements of leatherback turtles and how they affect their care in captivity will be discussed in this section.

1. Adaptations in Physiology

The extraordinary physiological adaptations that leatherback turtles possess allow them to live in a variety of maritime settings. Their leathery shell, which distinguishes them from other sea turtle species with hard, bony shells, is one of their most distinctive characteristics. Leatherbacks can dive to tremendous depths because of their flexible shell, which allows them to tolerate extreme pressure without breaking.

Furthermore, the streamlined body form of leatherback turtles allows them to swim effectively in open water. They can move through the water with amazing speed and agility thanks to their long, paddle-like front flippers. This adaptability is essential for traveling large marine stretches and hunting animals.

2. Control of temperature

Because they are ectothermic reptiles, leatherback turtles must obtain their body temperature from outside sources of heat. Reptiles need heat from the sun or their environment to sustain their metabolic processes, unlike mammals and birds who produce heat internally. Before entering deeper, colder waters, leatherbacks in the wild boost their body temperature by basking at the ocean's surface.

The health and welfare of leatherback turtles in captivity depend on the provision of the proper thermal gradient. To replicate the natural sunshine they would experience in their natural habitat, a basking area equipped with a heat lamp or heat pad should be made available. To make sure the temperature stays within the ideal range for thermoregulation, it is imperative to keep a careful eye on it.

3. Watery Setting

Because they are so well suited to a marine lifestyle, leatherback turtles live most of their lives in the ocean. During their annual migrations, they can cover thousands of kilometers and dive to depths of exceeding

1,000 meters (3,000 ft). The dynamic and vast character of the ocean habitat is difficult to replicate in captivity.

For captive leatherback turtles, a roomy tank or enclosure that allows for plenty of swimming space is necessary. The water must be kept at an appropriate temperature and salinity level and deep enough to permit unhindered flow. Offering a range of enrichment materials, such plants, rocks, and hiding places, can aid in simulating the intricacy of their native environment.

4. nutritional requirements

In the wild, jellyfish make up the majority of the diet of carnivorous leatherback turtles. They have unique characteristics that enable them to swallow their gelatinous prey whole, such as papillae lining their esophagus and neck. It might be difficult to replicate their natural diet in captivity because jellyfish can be hard to come by and keep healthy.

To address the nutritional demands of leatherback turtles kept in captivity, a diversified diet consisting of fish, squid, shrimp, and commercially available turtle pellets is required. To support their growth and general health, it's critical to provide a balanced meal with enough protein, vitamins, and minerals. To stop metabolic bone disease, it's also advised to add calcium and vitamin D3 supplements to their diet.

5. Nesting Patterns

The nesting habits of leatherback turtles are among their most amazing life features. Leatherback sea turtles are more globally distributed than other sea turtle species, which usually nest on tropical beaches. They can be found nesting on sandy shoreline all over the world.

Sometimes trekking thousands of kilometers to reach their nesting sites, female leatherbacks lay their eggs on the same beaches where they were born.

Replicating the conditions under which leatherback turtles nest in captivity is not possible since the turtles need access to the ocean and large stretches of sandy beach in order to lay their eggs. On the other hand, giving female turtles a nesting space with appropriate substrate—such as sand or soil—might promote their natural behaviors. During the nesting season, it is crucial to keep a constant eye on their activity and to offer suitable nesting chances.

6. Social Conduct

Most of the time, leatherback turtles are solitary creatures that only gather in groups for mating or when they are foraging in areas rich in prey. To avoid violence and guarantee that each turtle has enough room and resources, they should be kept apart in captivity. On the other hand, fostering social contact through shared areas or visual barriers can lessen boredom and improve the environment.

In summary

Giving leatherback turtles the attention and surroundings they need to flourish in captivity requires an understanding of their particular demands. We may contribute to ensuring their health and well-being by imitating elements of their natural habitat, such as temperature, water quality, and nutrition. But, taking care and responsibility when owning a pet is crucial, as leatherback turtles have intricate needs that must be satisfied to guarantee their long-term wellbeing.

Chapter 2

Creating the Ideal Habitat: Tank Needs and Interior Design

For the sake of a captive leatherback turtle's general health and well-being, an appropriate habitat must be created. For leatherback turtles to successfully replicate their native habitat, certain conditions must be fulfilled because they are aquatic reptiles. We will go over the tank specifications and décor in this section to make sure your leatherback turtle has the ideal home.

1. Dimensions & Size of the Tank

The size and dimensions of the tank or enclosure should be taken into account before anything else when building up a home for a leatherback turtle. The largest marine turtles, leatherbacks need plenty of room to swim and to move about comfortably. Generally speaking, the tank needs to be twice as wide and at least four times longer than the turtle's shell.

To ensure enough swimming room for adult leatherback turtles, a tank size of 500 gallons or greater is advised. Smaller tanks are suitable for housing juvenile turtles at first, but as they get bigger, larger enclosures will be needed. Making plans for the turtle's future growth and making sure the tank can hold their growing size are crucial.

2. Water Purity and Filtration

For captive leatherback turtles to remain healthy and happy, high water quality must be maintained. Numerous health difficulties, such as lung infections, stress-related illnesses, and shell rot, can be brought on by poor water quality. Reliability in water quality requires a strong filtering system.

It is recommended to use a high-quality canister or sump filter that can handle the amount of water in the tank. Regular water testing should also be carried out to keep an eye on variables including pH, ammonia, nitrite, and nitrate levels. To keep the turtle's habitat clean and healthy and to get rid of accumulated waste, water changes should be done on a regular basis.

3. Control of Temperature

The health and welfare of leatherback turtles depend on the water's temperature being kept at the proper level. Leatherbacks live in a variety of water temperatures in their natural habitat, which spans from tropical to temperate. Replicating the temperature range that the turtle would encounter in the wild is crucial for keeping it in captivity.

For leatherback turtles, the ideal water temperature range is 75°F to 85°F (24°C to 29°C). This can be achieved using a submersible aquarium heater. To guarantee that the heat is distributed evenly throughout the tank, the heater must be placed close to the filter's water intake. It's critical to regularly check the water's temperature to avoid swings that can put the turtle under stress.

4. Area of Basking

Leatherback turtles need access to a dry basking area where they can climb out of the water and thermoregulate in addition to swimming space. For leatherback turtles to increase body warmth and aid in digestion, they must bask. For their health and wellbeing, the tank must have a proper basking space.

Installing a dock or basking platform in the tank is a good idea. It should be made of non-toxic materials like acrylic or PVC. The platform should be placed beneath a heat lamp to offer warmth and should be big enough to comfortably fit the turtle's size. To guarantee that the turtle gets the UV rays required for vitamin D production, a UVB lamp should also be supplied.

5. Substance

While adding a substrate can assist recreate the natural environment and enrich the turtle, it is not a strict requirement for leatherback turtle aquariums. The tank's bottom can be made to look realistic by using a substrate like gravel or fine sand. It is imperative to select a substrate that is both easily cleaned and safe for the turtle.

Before adding substrate to the tank, it should be well washed to get rid of any pollutants or dirt. To stop trash and bacteria from building up, it's also critical to clean and replace the substrate on a regular basis. As an alternative, bare-bottom tanks can be utilized; these are simpler to maintain but could not offer the turtle as much enrichment.

6. Accents and Enhancements

The leatherback turtle can have a dynamic and interesting environment in the tank with the addition of décor and enrichment items. Caves, driftwood, rocks, and artificial plants can all offer turtles places to hide and explore. To protect the turtle from harm, it is imperative that you select décor pieces that are rounded, smooth, and devoid of sharp edges.

In addition, the presence of buoys or logs that float can promote diving and sunbathing, two natural activities. Periodically changing the décor can also assist keep a turtle from becoming bored and encourage its innate tendencies. But it's crucial to keep a careful eye on the turtle's activities and take out any objects that could entangle or be ingested.

7. Observation and upkeep

The health and welfare of the leatherback turtle depend on routine care and observation once the habitat has been established. It is important to carry out daily duties including feeding, testing the water, and keeping an eye on the temperature constantly. It is also recommended to perform weekly tank cleanings and water changes in order to get rid of trash and debris and stop dangerous germs from growing.

It's also critical to pay great attention to the turtle's behavior to spot any indications of stress, disease, or injury. Any changes in appearance, activity level, or appetite should be quickly addressed to avoid the emergence of more serious health problems. You can make sure your captive leatherback turtle has a healthy and stimulating habitat by giving it careful attention.

In summary

A leatherback turtle's particular demands and preferences must be carefully taken into account when creating the ideal home for them. Your turtle can live in a dynamic and engaging environment if you give it a large tank with clean water, the right temperature, and enriching décor. Maintaining the health and welfare of your leatherback turtle for many years to come requires routine observation and care.

Chapter 3

Feeding Your Leatherback Turtle: Crucial Food and Diet

A leatherback turtle's dietary and nutritional demands must be carefully considered when feeding it in captivity. Since they are carnivorous reptiles, leatherback turtles have adapted to live mostly on jellyfish in the wild. To maintain their health and wellbeing, it can be difficult to replicate their natural diet in captivity; therefore, a diversified and balanced approach is needed. We will go over all the important details of feeding a leatherback turtle in this detailed guide, including what they should eat, how often to feed them, and whether or not to use nutritional supplements.

1. Recognizing Leatherback Turtles' Natural Diet

Leatherback turtles are specialized predators that mostly eat jellyfish in their natural habitat. Their special morphology and physiology allow them to effectively catch, swallow, and digest these gelatinous prey objects. Specialized papillae lining their esophagus and neck enable leatherback turtles to grasp and swallow slippery prey.

Although jellyfish make up the majority of their diet, fish, squid, crabs, and mollusks can also be eaten by leatherback turtles when the opportunity arises. However, because of their abundance in the maritime environment, jellyfish continue to be their preferred and most important source of sustenance.

2. Reproducing in Captivity a Natural Diet

It can be difficult to replicate the natural diet of leatherback turtles in captivity since jellyfish can be hard to come by and keep as a reliable food supply. Furthermore, feeding a diet made entirely of jellyfish would not give all the necessary elements for optimum health and wellbeing.

It's crucial to offer a range of prey items that closely resemble the nutritional makeup of their natural diet in order to guarantee a balanced and nutrient-rich diet. A mix of fish, squid, shrimp, and commercially available turtle pellets made especially for aquatic turtles may be included in this.

3. Appropriate Diet for Leatherback Turtles

It is crucial to choose wholesome, fresh, and nutrient-dense prey items for your leatherback turtle that are devoid of pollutants and parasites. Fish that can be served whole or as fillets, such mackerel, herring, and tilapia, are great providers of protein and important fatty acids.

Shrimp and squid are also very nutrient-dense prey items that offer vital vitamins and minerals, including as calcium and phosphorus, which are critical for the health of the shell and bones. It is possible to present these prey items whole or sliced into portions that suit the turtle's eating habits.

The diet of the turtle may also include commercially available pellets made especially for aquatic turtles. With a balanced mix of protein, vitamins, and minerals, these pellets are made to fulfill the dietary requirements of turtles kept in captivity. They should, however, be supplemented with a range of fresh prey items and should not be the exclusive source of sustenance.

4. Feeding Quantities and Frequency

For example, age, size, activity level, and metabolic rate can all affect how often and how much a leatherback turtle eats. While adult turtles may need fewer feedings, juveniles usually need more regular feedings to maintain their growth and development.

Juvenile leatherback turtles should generally be fed every day, with portion quantities being modified according to size and hunger. Adult turtles can be fed several times a week or every other day, depending on how much food they require in each particular meal. To avoid under- or overfeeding your turtle, it's critical to keep a constant eye on its body condition and modify the frequency and size of its meals properly.

5. Supplements for Nutrition

To make sure their nutritional demands are satisfied, leatherback turtles may need to take extra vitamins and minerals in addition to a diversified diet of prey items. For the health of their shells and bones, in particular, calcium and vitamin D3 should be given as part of their diet.

To guarantee sufficient calcium intake, commercial calcium supplements made especially for reptiles can be sprinkled into prey items prior to feeding. Supplementing with vitamin D3 may also be important, particularly for turtles that are not regularly exposed to UVB lights or natural sunlight.

6. Feeding Techniques and Enhancement

To encourage natural eating patterns and mental stimulation, it's crucial to use enrichment activities and feeding tactics in addition to offering a varied food and nutritional supplements. Scatter feeding can assist arouse the natural hunting and foraging impulses of the turtle by dispersing prey items across the tank.

Feeding enrichment toys, including floating items that dispense food when touched or puzzle feeders, can also stimulate the mind and promote exercise. To guarantee the turtles' involvement and wellbeing, it's critical to keep an eye on their behavior during feeding and modify enrichment activities as necessary.

7. In summary

A leatherback turtle's dietary and nutritional demands must be carefully considered when feeding it in captivity. Your turtle will get the nutrition it needs to flourish in captivity if you feed it a diversified diet of high-quality prey items supplemented with vital vitamins and minerals. To further enhance their general health and wellbeing, feeding strategies and enrichment activities can encourage natural feeding behaviors and cerebral stimulation. The dietary requirements of leatherback turtles must be given first priority by conscientious pet owners, and they must also receive the care and attention necessary for them to enjoy long, healthy lives in captivity.

Chapter 4

Sustaining Optimal Health: Typical Health Problems and Treatment Advice

In order to guarantee the best possible health for a leatherback turtle kept in captivity, proactive care and routine observation are necessary. Even though these magnificent animals are tough, they can suffer from a number of illnesses, such as nutritional deficits and infections of the shell. We will examine the common health problems that may impact leatherback turtles kept in captivity in this extensive guide, along with helpful maintenance advice.

1. Infections with Shells

Shell infections are among the most frequent health problems that leatherback turtles face. These infections can be brought on by trauma, poor water quality, or insufficient basking opportunities. The presence of lesions, discolouration, or abnormal growths on the turtle's shell are indicative of shell infections.

Maintaining excellent water quality and offering a clean, dry basking place where the turtle may thermoregulate and dry off entirely are crucial for preventing shell infections. To get rid of waste and debris that can encourage the growth of bacteria in tanks, regular tank cleanings and water changes are crucial.

It's critical to get veterinarian care as soon as possible if a shell infection is detected. In order to treat bacterial infections, treatment may include systemic or topical antibiotics as well as supportive care to encourage healing and avert additional issues.

2. infections of the respiratory system

Another common health problem that can affect leatherback turtles kept in captivity is respiratory infections, especially if their habitat is neglected or if they are subjected to environmental stressors. Lethargy, difficulty breathing, wheezing, and nasal discharge are some of the symptoms of respiratory infections.

Maintaining ideal water quality and temperature is crucial for preventing respiratory infections. Adequate ventilation in the tank is also necessary to avoid the growth of mold and humidity. Make sure the turtle always has access to clean, oxygenated water by keeping the tank from becoming too crowded.

Timely veterinarian care is crucial if a respiratory illness is suspected. Antibiotics for bacterial infections and supportive care for symptom relief and immune system support may be part of the treatment plan for the turtle.

3. Inadequate Nutrients

If leatherback turtles are not fed a balanced, diverse diet that satisfies their unique dietary needs, nutritional deficits may result. Calcium, vitamin D3, and vitamin A deficits are common nutritional inadequacies in captive turtles.

A varied diet of high-quality prey items, supplemented with vital vitamins and minerals as needed, is crucial to preventing nutritional deficits. While vitamin D3 supplements could be required for turtles that aren't frequently exposed to UVB lamps or natural sunshine, calcium supplements can be sprinkled onto prey items to ensure proper calcium intake.

To keep an eye on the turtle's general health and nutritional state, routine veterinary examinations are crucial. Blood tests can be used to measure calcium, vitamin D3, and other vital nutrient levels. If deficits are found, these tests can help with early detection and treatment.

4. Parasitic Diseases

In captivity, leatherback turtles are susceptible to parasitic illnesses, especially if they live in unsuitable conditions or are exposed to tainted water sources. Internal parasites like nematodes, cestodes, and protozoa as well as external parasites like ticks and mites are common parasites that can harm leatherback turtles.

Maintaining excellent water quality and cleanliness in the tank, together with routine veterinary check-ups to look for indications of parasite infestation, are critical to preventing parasitic diseases. Preventing the spread of parasites can also be achieved by quarantining newly acquired turtles prior to releasing them into an established population.

In the event that a parasitic infection is suspected, it is imperative to swiftly seek veterinarian care. In order to relieve symptoms and avoid complications, treatment may include supportive care, antiparasitic drugs, or deworming therapies.

5. Trauma and Damage

It is possible for leatherback turtles to sustain trauma and injuries, especially if they live in an environment with sharp objects or hostile tankmates. Cuts, abrasions, shell fractures, and soft tissue injuries are examples of common injuries.

It is crucial to give the turtle a safe and secure habitat that is devoid of potential risks or sharp objects in order to prevent trauma and injuries. Aggressive people should be housed apart to prevent injuries, and tankmates should be carefully chosen to assure compatibility.

In the event that a turtle is hurt, it's critical to get veterinarian attention as away. Debridement and cleaning of the wounds may be part of the treatment, in addition to pain control and supportive care to encourage recovery.

6. Behavioral Problems

In captivity, leatherback turtles may also exhibit behavioral problems like aggression, tension, and boredom, especially if their social and environmental demands are not sufficiently satisfied. Aggression toward tankmates, extensive hiding, or repetitive behaviors like pacing or self-harming are examples of behavioral disorders.

A dynamic and enriching habitat, with lots of room for swimming and exploration, social interaction chances, and mental stimulation, is crucial for preventing behavioral problems in turtles. Having hiding places, floating items, and stimulating activities available can help people decompress and feel less stressed.

It's critical to evaluate the turtle's surroundings and make the necessary changes to address any underlying causes if behavioral problems continue. Developing a behavior modification strategy specific to the needs of the turtle may also benefit from speaking with a veterinarian or reptile behavior specialist.

7. In summary

A leatherback turtle kept in captivity needs proactive management and routine observation to remain in optimal health. You can contribute to ensuring that your turtle is healthy and happy for many years to come by treating common health issues such shell infections, respiratory infections, nutritional deficiencies, parasite infections, trauma, and behavioral issues. It is imperative that we, as conscientious pet owners, give the health and welfare of leatherback turtles top priority and give them the love and care they need to flourish in captivity. A thorough care plan for leatherback turtles should include regular veterinary examinations, appropriate diet, a clean and stimulating environment, and close observation. Leatherback turtles can live long, healthy lives in captivity with the right care and attention, delighting and fascinating their keepers.

Chapter 5

Taking Care of and Having Safe Contacts with Your Leatherback Turtle

Respecting the natural requirements and habits of a leatherback turtle necessitates careful handling. These amazing animals may appear submissive, but they are wild animals with needs that must be met for their survival. We'll go over the best ways to handle and interact with your leatherback turtle securely in this extensive guide, along with some advice on how to keep yourself and the turtle from getting hurt.

1. Comprehending the Behavior of Leatherback Turtles

It's important to comprehend a leatherback turtle's natural behaviors and reactions to various stimuli before attempting to manage one. Most of the time, leatherback turtles are lonely creatures who spend their time swimming and searching the ocean for food. They can move swiftly on land and in the water because they have strong limbs and are excellent swimmers.

Leatherback turtles kept in captivity may engage in activities like swimming, eating, exploring their surroundings, and basking. If they sense danger or insecurity, they may also show symptoms of stress or discomfort, such as pulling their head and limbs under their shell or making an effort to break free from handling.

2. Reducing Stress

In order to protect and preserve the wellbeing of a leatherback turtle, it is imperative to minimize stress when working with them. The immune system of turtles can be weakened by stress, leaving them more vulnerable to illness and disease. It's critical to handle the turtle softly and carefully to reduce stress; avoid startling them with abrupt movements or loud noises.

Furthermore, it's crucial to restrict handling to essential duties like moving the turtle for medical attention or maintaining its habitat. Prolonged or excessive handling might result in excessive stress, which over time may produce behavioral difficulties or health issues.

3. Managing Methods

It's crucial to employ the right handling methods when working with leatherback turtles to protect them and you. Large and strong, leatherback turtles must be handled carefully to prevent damage. The following advice can help you handle a leatherback turtle safely:

- To avoid frightening the turtle, approach it quietly and slowly.

- Using both hands, support the turtle's body by placing one under the front and the other under the back.

- Take care when lifting the turtle so as not to press on its shell or limbs.

- The turtle may get hurt or stressed if you lift it by its flippers.

- To avoid falls or mishaps, keep the turtle near the ground or a sturdy surface.

- Return the turtle to its enclosure as quickly as you can; try not to handle it for long.

4. Getting to Know Your Leatherback Turtle

There are various ways to engage with your leatherback turtle that can improve their wellbeing and deepen your relationship, even if handling should be minimized. The following are a few secure and entertaining ways to communicate with your leatherback turtle:

Observing their behavior: To find out more about your turtle's routines and preferences, spend some time watching how they behave in their cage. By doing so, you will be better able to meet their requirements and give them the attention they need.

Feeding: You can interact with the turtle during feeding time by giving it prey by hand or using enrichment tools. Just take care not to place your fingers too near the turtle's mouth to avoid unintentional bites.

Activities for enrichment: Giving the turtle access to floating objects, puzzle feeders, and hiding places can promote natural behaviors and mental stimulation. For you and the turtle, interacting with these enrichment materials can be enjoyable and fulfilling.

5. Safety Measures

It's crucial to follow the right safety procedures when interacting with a leatherback turtle to avoid mishaps or injury. When handled carelessly, leatherback turtles can be dangerous due to their strong limbs and sharp beaks. The following safety measures should be remembered:

- To stop the transmission of bacteria or parasites, make sure you thoroughly wash your hands both before and after handling the turtle.
- Refrain from handling the turtle if you are ill or if your hands are wounded or injured in any way.
- To avoid mishaps or injury, keep small children and dogs away from the turtle's enclosure.
- Never try to saddle or ride a turtle as this might stress out the creature and lead to damage.

- Release the turtle gently and give it time to calm down if it shows indications of distress or aggression, like snapping or hissing.

6. Enhancement of Environment

For the wellbeing of leatherback turtles kept in captivity, environmental enrichment is just as important as safe handling and engagement. Boredom and tension can be decreased, physical activity can be encouraged, and natural behaviors can be stimulated with enrichment activities. The following are some suggestions for improving the leatherback turtles' surroundings:

- Give the turtle floating items to explore and engage with, such logs, plants, or buoys.
- providing caves or hiding places where the turtle can go to feel safe and comfortable.

- To offer variety and excitement, rearrange décor and enrichment materials on a regular basis.
- Including foraging activities or puzzle feeders to promote natural hunting and feeding habits.

7. In summary

Patience, consideration, and respect for the natural requirements and habits of your leatherback turtle are necessary for handling and engaging with it properly. You may guarantee a happy and fulfilling experience for both you and the turtle by being aware of the habits of leatherback turtles, reducing stress, employing suitable handling skills, and adopting the necessary safety precautions. The well-being and quality of life of a turtle kept in captivity can be further improved by offering opportunities for interaction and environmental enrichment. Your leatherback turtle can have a long and happy life if given the proper care and attention.

Chapter 6

Breeding Factors and Conscientious Ownership

The process of breeding leatherback turtles in captivity is intricate and difficult, requiring knowledge, preparation, and adherence to moral and legal guidelines. While breeding programs can aid in conservation efforts and advance scientific understanding of these amazing animals, it is crucial to put the welfare of the turtles first and make sure that breeding practices are morally and responsibly carried out. We shall examine the many factors and duties related to breeding leatherback turtles in captivity in this extensive tutorial.

1. Recognizing the Reproduction of Leatherback Turtles

The remarkable reproductive habits of leatherback turtles are well known. These behaviors include synchronized nesting events on sandy beaches as well as long-distance migrations between feeding and breeding areas. Natal homing is the process by which female leatherback turtles lay their eggs on the beaches where they were born. Females excavate sand nests during nesting season, where they lay clutches of eggs that take about two months to hatch.

It is difficult to replicate the nesting and breeding habits of leatherback turtles in captivity since it need for large areas, specialized infrastructure, and cautious environmental management. However, effective breeding programs can be built to support conservation efforts and further scientific knowledge of leatherback turtle reproduction with the right planning and knowledge.

2. Moral Aspects to Take into Account

It's important to think through the moral obligations and ramifications of captive breeding before starting a leatherback turtle breeding program. As an endangered species, leatherback turtles are threatened by a variety of factors in the wild, such as poaching, pollution, habitat loss, and climate change. By ensuring populations and bolstering conservation efforts, captive turtle breeding can help lessen some of these risks. Prioritizing the turtles' well-being and making ensuring that breeding operations are carried out in an ethical and responsible manner are crucial, nevertheless.

The following moral guidelines ought to be followed by conscientious breeding programs:

- regard for the turtles' natural needs and behaviors.

- dedication to the long-term viability of captive populations and genetic diversity.

- Accountability and openness in breeding procedures and decision-making.

- cooperation with regulatory bodies and conservation organizations to guarantee adherence to laws and best practices.

3. Legal Aspects to Take into Account

Since leatherback turtles are protected by both national and international laws and treaties, breeding them in captivity is subject to a number of legal restrictions and permit requirements. It's crucial to become familiar with the applicable legal frameworks and secure any licenses or permits needed for breeding, research, or teaching operations before starting a breeding program.

The Endangered Species Act (ESA), which forbids the taking, harassment, or damage of leatherback turtles and their habitats, provides protection for leatherback turtles in the United States. Permits from the US may be needed for breeding initiatives. Fish and Wildlife Service (USFWS) or other oversight organizations to guarantee adherence to ESA guidelines.

The International Union for Conservation of Nature (IUCN) has classified leatherback turtles as critically endangered globally, and they are protected by the Convention on International Trade in Endangered Species of Wild Fauna and Flora (CITES). To guarantee conformity with international standards, breeding operations requiring cross-border collaboration or the transfer of turtles may need permits or authorization from CITES authorities.

4. Facilities Needed

A breeding program for leatherback turtles needs to be established, and this involves specialist facilities that can offer the right habitat and environmental conditions for nesting, breeding, and egg incubation. Important facility specifications could be:

- large outdoor cages with soil or sand access for nest building.
- indoor habitats with controlled temperatures where turtles are kept when they are not nesting.
- hatcheries or incubation chambers with humidity and temperature controls.
- quarantine zones with health surveillance for recent arrivals.
- Veterinary clinics and personnel with expertise in caring for and handling reptiles.

The safety and wellbeing of the turtles should be the top priority while designing a facility. Features like safe cages, realistic habitat elements, and enrichment opportunities should be included to encourage the turtles' natural behaviors and general well-being.

5. Management of Breeding

It takes careful control of breeding partners, mating behavior, nesting, and egg incubation to successfully breed leatherback turtles in captivity. Experienced biologists, vets, and husbandry personnel with training in reptile reproduction and breeding management are essential to the success of breeding projects.

Reproductive health, compatibility, and genetic variety should all be taken into consideration when choosing breeding pairings. Outside of the breeding season, male and female turtles should be kept apart to avoid aggressive behavior and to guarantee appropriate training prior to mating efforts.

Male and female turtles may be introduced for controlled mating during the breeding season. Breeding management decisions can be influenced by observing courtship displays, copulation attempts, and mating behavior. These observations can assist assess the success of mating.

After mating, female turtles need to have access to sand or dirt for digging nests, as well as appropriate nesting environment. To reduce predation and guarantee the best hatch rates, nesting activity should be continuously observed, and eggs should be quickly gathered for artificial incubation.

6. Incubation of Eggs

In order to ensure a successful hatch, egg incubation is a crucial step in the breeding process that requires careful control of temperature, humidity, and ventilation. The sex ratio of hatchlings is influenced by temperature-dependent sex determination, and leatherback turtle eggs normally incubate for 60 to 70 days.

Precise temperature control systems are essential for hatcheries and incubators to provide a consistent temperature within the range that is best for the development of embryos. In order to avoid fungal development or desiccation, humidity levels should also be checked and changed as necessary.

Eggs should be often checked for developmental indicators during incubation, such as blood vessel creation and embryo movement. To increase hatch rates, eggs exhibiting signs of discomfort or aberrant development might need to get extra attention or intervention.

7. Care for Hatchlings

Another crucial component of breeding management is hatchling care, which calls for specific facilities and husbandry techniques to guarantee the wellbeing and survival of young turtles. It is recommended that hatchlings be kept in temperature-controlled spaces with availability to fresh water and suitable prey for nourishment.

Small fish, shrimp, and squid can be included in a hatchling's diet, along with commercial turtle pellets made specifically for young turtles. A balanced food that satisfies the nutritional requirements of developing hatchlings and fosters healthy development should be carefully provided.

For hatchling turtles, regular health monitoring and veterinarian care are crucial. Growth rates, feeding habits, and general condition should all be taken into consideration. As they could be more susceptible to illness, predators, and environmental stressors, hatchlings should be raised in a secure and nurturing setting to ensure their wellbeing.

8. Implications for Conservation

In addition to improving scientific understanding and increasing public awareness of the suffering of endangered species, breeding leatherback turtles in captivity can have a substantial positive impact on conservation. By doing research on reproductive biology and behavior, producing assurance populations for upcoming reintroduction efforts, and involving the public in outreach and education campaigns on conservation, ethical breeding projects can promote conservation initiatives.

It's crucial to understand, though, that captive breeding cannot take the place of wild conservation efforts. The long-term survival of the leatherback turtle species depends on initiatives to preserve its habitat, lessen threats from human activity, and support sustainable fisheries management.

9. Conscientious Ownership

When breeding leatherback turtles in captivity, appropriate ownership is crucial, just like in any undertaking involving the care and control of living organisms. Being a responsible owner means:

- putting the turtles' welfare and health above all else.
- following the law and ethical guidelines for husbandry and breeding.
- pledging to provide the turtles with ongoing care and assistance for the duration of their lives.

- working together to promote the preservation of leatherback turtles and their ecosystems with regulatory bodies, other stakeholders, and conservation organizations.

- It takes commitment, knowledge, and money to guarantee that breeding programs are run in a way that benefits turtles and advances their conservation when it comes to responsible ownership.

10. In summary

The process of breeding leatherback turtles in captivity is intricate and difficult, requiring knowledge, preparation, and adherence to moral and legal guidelines. While breeding programs can aid in conservation efforts and advance scientific understanding of these amazing animals, it is crucial to put the welfare of the turtles first and make sure that breeding practices are morally and responsibly carried out. Responsible breeders can significantly aid in the conservation of this critically endangered species by adopting proper husbandry techniques, working with regulatory agencies and conservation organizations, and learning about the natural needs and behaviors of leatherback turtles. We can work together to ensure a better future for leatherback turtles and their ecosystems if we are dedicated, compassionate, and committed.

Chapter 7

Common Questions Concerning the Care of Leatherback Turtle Pets

Although owning a leatherback turtle as a pet can be gratifying, there are particular difficulties and duties involved. Prospective turtle owners frequently have a lot of questions about how to take care of these interesting creatures, from tank setup to nutritional requirements. We'll answer some of the most common queries on owning leatherback turtles as pets in this guide, offering insightful commentary and helpful pointers for would-be turtle owners.

1. What prerequisites must a person meet in order to maintain a leatherback turtle as a pet?

A leatherback turtle's unique needs must be carefully considered before keeping one as a pet. A large tank with enough of swimming room, a UVB-lit basking area, a diverse diet of prey items, and routine maintenance of water quality and temperature are all basic needs. Furthermore, owners need to be ready to offer enrichment activities that will enhance the physical and mental health of their turtles.

2. What size tank is necessary for a leatherback turtle?

The largest kind of sea turtles, leatherbacks need a large tank to fit their bulk. Generally speaking, the tank needs to be twice as wide and at least four times longer than the turtle's shell. To ensure enough swimming room for adult leatherback turtles, a tank size of 500 gallons or greater is advised.

3. What kind of food is best for a leatherback turtle?

In the wild, leatherback turtles are carnivorous reptiles that eat mostly jellyfish. A diversified diet consisting of prey items including fish, squid, shrimp, and commercially available turtle pellets should be given to captive animals. A balanced meal that satisfies the turtle's need for protein, vitamins, and minerals is crucial.

4. Do leatherback turtles require a place to bask?

Yes, in order for them to climb out of the water and maintain their body temperature, leatherback turtles need to have access to a dry basking place. For leatherback turtles to increase body warmth and aid in digestion, they must bask. Installing a dock or basking platform in the tank is recommended, especially beneath a heat lamp and UVB lamp to supply warmth and UV light for the production of vitamin D.

5. How frequently should the tank of my leatherback turtle be cleaned?

Leatherback turtle health and wellbeing depend on regular tank care. Weekly water changes are necessary to keep the quality of the water at its best and to remove waste and debris. Furthermore, it is imperative to periodically clean or replace the filters in order to guarantee optimal filtration and water movement within the tank.

6. Can leatherback turtles coexist with fish or other turtles?

Being solitary creatures, leatherback turtles can act aggressively toward tankmates, particularly if they sense danger or insecurity. It is generally not advised to keep leatherback turtles in the same enclosure as fish or other turtles since disputes over food, territory, and sunbathing areas may occur. In order to reduce stress and shield leatherback turtles from harm, as well as other tankmates, it is best to give them their own area.

7. Do any unique lighting or heating requirements exist for leatherback turtles?

In order to meet their physiological needs, leatherback turtles do indeed need access to UVB lighting and heat lamps. The creation of vitamin D, which is required for calcium metabolism and shell health, depends on UVB sunshine. Warmth from heat lamps aids in keeping the turtle's body temperature in the ideal range for metabolism and digestion. For the turtle's general health and well-being, a basking area with sufficient UVB illumination and heating is important.

8. What is the lifespan of a leatherback turtle?

Reptiles having a lifetime of several decades or more are leatherback turtles. Leatherback turtles have a 50-year lifespan in the wild, and with the right care and handling, they can live even longer in captivity. A well-balanced diet, frequent veterinarian care, and an appropriate habitat can all help extend the lives of leatherback turtles kept in captivity.

9. Is it acceptable to own leatherback turtles as pets?

Depending on the jurisdiction and area, owning leatherback turtles as pets has different legal statuses. It may be against the law to own or maintain leatherback turtles as pets in some locations due to national or international laws and regulations protecting these animals. It's crucial to learn about and abide by any local laws or regulations before obtaining a leatherback turtle as a pet.

10. If I am unable to care for my leatherback turtle, may I release it back into the wild?

It is generally not advised to release captive-bred leatherback turtles into the wild since they might not have the instincts and survival skills needed to survive in their native environment. Furthermore, releasing captive turtles into the wild has the potential to disturb local ecosystems and spread diseases or parasites to wild populations. It's best to find a suitable adopter who can offer appropriate care and accommodations for your leatherback turtle, or to rehome it with a reputable rescue organization, if you are unable to continue caring for it.

11. How can I determine the health of my leatherback turtle?

It's critical to keep an eye on your leatherback turtle's health in order to identify and address any problems early on. A smooth, undamaged shell, bright, attentive behavior, clear, brilliant eyes, vigorous swimming and feeding habits, and frequent basking are all indicators of a healthy leatherback turtle. Any alterations in the animal's appearance, behavior, or appetite should be immediately addressed, and veterinarian care should be sought if required.

12. Are pet leatherback turtles a good choice?

Some pet owners may not be able to provide the particular care and habitat needs that leatherback turtles require. For seasoned reptile lovers, they can make fascinating and fulfilling pets, but beginners or those who are not knowledgeable with their particular requirements shouldn't have one. To maintain the health and well-being of leatherback turtles, proper care and maintenance take commitment, time, and resources.

In summary

For those who are prepared to give their leatherback turtles the requisite care and attention to suit their individual needs, owning them as pets may be a fulfilling experience. Prospective owners can create an appropriate habitat where these gorgeous creatures can thrive by knowing the fundamentals of housing, feeding, and caring for leatherback turtles. Before committing, though, it's important to learn about and weigh the obligations and difficulties that come with owning leatherback turtles as pets. Leatherback turtles can provide their owners with joy and intrigue for many years to come if they are given the right care and ownership.